JUST **100** CALORIES

JUST 100 CALORIES

Love Food™ is an imprint of
Parragon Books Ltd

Parragon
Queen Street House
4 Queen Street
Bath BA1 1HE, UK

Love Food™ and the accompanying heart
device is a trade mark of Parragon Books Ltd

Design: Terry Jeavons & Company
Photographer: Mike Cooper
Home economist: Lincoln Jefferson

ISBN 978-1-4054-8776-4

Printed in China

This book uses metric and imperial
measurements. Follow the same units of
measurement throughout; do not mix metric
and imperial. All spoon measurements are
level, unless otherwise stated: teaspoons
are assumed to be 5ml, and tablespoons
are assumed to be 15ml. Unless otherwise
stated, milk is assumed to be full fat, eggs
and individual fruits such as bananas are
medium, and pepper is freshly ground
black pepper.

Recipes using raw or very lightly cooked eggs
should be avoided by children, the elderly,
pregnant women, convalescents, and anyone
suffering from an illness. Pregnant and
breast-feeding women are advised to avoid
eating peanuts and peanut products.

Contents

Introduction

Today's lifestyle is not conducive to healthy eating. It is all too easy to snack on convenience foods, especially when on the move. Bingeing when you are starving-hungry is the classic way to pile on the pounds and, before you know where you are, you are far larger than you would wish to be. But how can this change? There is a host of diet books on the market, each one promising that it has the answer – low carbohydrate, high protein, microbiotic or Glycaemic Index (GI). So, we lurch from one diet to another in a desperate struggle to get on top of the problem. We all know that to enjoy a balanced diet we need to cut out the fat and to eat lots more fruit, vegetables and fibre. But what does that mean, and how do we know if we are achieving this?

The simple fact is that the more calories that are consumed, the greater the amount of food that is stored in the body as fat, no matter where those excess calories come from. In the West we tend to eat far too many calories – for most healthy women the daily requirement is no more than 2,000 calories, while healthy men require no more than 2,500 calories per day. (This does not apply to manual workers.) In order to lose weight you have to reduce the amount of calories consumed. The recommended daily amount of calories for women in order to lose weight is 1,500 and for men it is 2,000. Any balanced weight loss programme should also include regular exercise.

Children, because they are growing and are often far more active than adults, require a good proportion of their calories from high energy-giving foods, such as slow-releasing complex carbohydrates like vegetables, fruits, pulses and wholewheat products, plus, of course, a good proportion of protein, including fish, poultry and lean meat, and also a certain amount of products containing fat. All these foods contain important minerals such as calcium, which is vital for growth. As we grow older, the body's metabolism slows down and so fewer calories are required. The one to watch is fat. This contains twice as many calories as any other food. One gram of carbohydrate or protein is 4 calories while 1 gram of fat is 9 calories.

This book is designed in a practical way to stop the yo-yo effect of weight loss and weight gain, with recipes that are calorie-counted so you can see at a glance exactly how many calories there are in each portion. Each recipe is easy to prepare and cook and will help you control your intake and maintain a balanced diet. There are some spicy fish dishes, exotic chicken meals as well as some favourite meat recipes, but don't despair, if you have a sweet tooth there are a few little gems together with some healthy drinks and the occasional treat of a glass or two of cheer. So get counting and cooking and see how easy it is to maintain a healthy and balanced diet.

1 Breakfast & Brunches

There are plenty of recipes within this chapter to tempt and delight without piling on the calories, ranging from Melon & Strawberry Crunch, a delicious start to any morning and is simply bursting with fruit, to Smoked Salmon Scramble or tasty Hot Garlic-stuffed Mushrooms, perfect for a lazy Sunday brunch.

Melon & Strawberry Crunch

serves 4
calories per portion

98

not including orange juice or milk

INGREDIENTS

25 g/1 oz rolled oats

25 g/1 oz oat bran

2 tbsp toasted flaked almonds

25 g/1 oz ready-to-eat dried apricots, finely chopped

½ melon, such as Galia

225 g/8 oz strawberries

150 ml/5 fl oz orange juice or skimmed milk, to serve (optional)

1 Put the rolled oats and oat bran in a bowl and stir in the almonds and dried apricots.

2 Discard the skin and seeds from the melon and cut into small bite-sized pieces. Halve the strawberries if large.

3 Divide the rolled oat mixture between 4 individual bowls then top with the fruits. If liked, serve with either skimmed milk or orange juice.

Asparagus with Tomato & Bacon

INGREDIENTS

serves 4
calories per
portion

74

350 g/12 oz fresh asparagus spears

four x 115 g/4 oz lean back bacon rashers or 4 thin slices Parma ham

4 medium tomatoes

pepper

1 Trim off the woody part of the asparagus stems and discard. Using a vegetable peeler, peel the spears in a downward action to remove any other woody parts.

2 Bring a large frying pan half-filled with water to the boil (or use a steamer). Add the asparagus to the boiling water and cook for 5–6 minutes, or until tender. Drain and keep warm.

3 Meanwhile, preheat the grill and line the grill rack with foil. Put the bacon rashers on the foil-lined grill rack. Cut the tomatoes in half and place these on the grill rack. Grill for 4–5 minutes, or until the bacon is crisp. Turn the bacon over halfway through cooking. If using Parma ham, there is no need to cook it.

4 Divide the asparagus, bacon and tomatoes between four plates. To serve, sprinkle the tomatoes with pepper, to taste.

Grapefruit Cups

INGREDIENTS

serves 4
calories
per half

78

2 red or pink grapefruit, about
450 g/1 lb each

25 g/1 oz Demerara sugar

2 ripe passion fruit or 2 tbsp
orange flower water

1 Preheat the grill to medium and line the grill rack with foil. Cut the grapefruits in half and, using a grapefruit knife or small, sharp-pointed knife, carefully loosen the segments and remove the central piece of pith. Carefully cut under the segments to make them easier to remove.

2 Put the grapefruit on the foil-lined rack and sprinkle with the sugar. Cook under the grill for 5 minutes, or until the sugar has melted.

3 If using passion fruit, scoop out the seeds and flesh, and spoon over the cooked grapefruit. Alternatively, pour over the orange flower water. Serve half a grapefruit per person while still hot.

Wake-up Kebabs

INGREDIENTS

serves 4
calories per
kebab

61

½ red apple, cored and sliced

1 large banana, peeled and cut into bite-sized pieces

1 tbsp orange or lemon juice

1 large watermelon wedge, peeled, deseeded and cut into small chunks

1 melon wedge, such as Ogen or Galia, peeled, deseeded and cut into small chunks

8 fresh strawberries

2 tsp clear honey

1 Preheat the grill to high and line the grill rack with foil. Brush the apple and banana with the orange or lemon juice.

2 Thread the melon, apple, banana and strawberries onto 4 kebab sticks or presoaked wooden skewers and place on the grill rack.

3 Drizzle with the honey then grill for 5–6 minutes, turning the kebabs over halfway through cooking. Serve while warm.

Oven-baked Eggs with Tomato Salsa

serves 4
calories per
portion

93

INGREDIENTS

FOR THE SALSA

2 ripe tomatoes, finely
chopped

3 spring onions, trimmed
and finely chopped

2.5-cm/1-inch piece cucumber,
finely chopped

Tabasco sauce, to taste

1 tbsp chopped fresh coriander

FOR THE EGGS

4 sprays olive oil

4 eggs

pepper

1 Preheat the oven to 180°C/350°F/Gas Mark 4.
To prepare the salsa, put the tomatoes, spring
onions, cucumber and Tabasco sauce in a small
saucepan and set aside.

2 Lightly spray 4 ramekins with oil and place
a spoonful of the prepared salsa in the base of
each dish. Carefully break an egg into each
ramekin dish. Place the dishes in a roasting tin
half-filled with hot water and sprinkle the top
of each egg with pepper. Heat the remaining
salsa in the saucepan gently.

3 Bake the eggs for 8–12 minutes, or until
cooked to personal preference. Stir the
chopped coriander into the reserved salsa
and serve with the cooked eggs.

Smoked Salmon Scramble

INGREDIENTS

serves 4
calories per
portion

92

4 tomatoes, about 115 g/4 oz each

55 g/2 oz smoked salmon pieces

2 eggs

1 egg white

1 tbsp water

pepper

1 tbsp snipped fresh chives, for sprinkling

1 Preheat the grill to high and line the grill rack with foil. Cut the tomatoes in half and scoop out the flesh and seeds. Chop the flesh finely then place in a sieve to allow the excess liquid to drain away.

2 Cut the smoked salmon into small pieces. In a separate bowl, beat the eggs, egg white and water, with pepper to taste. Heat a non-stick small saucepan and when hot, add the beaten egg. Cook for 1 minute, stirring constantly, then stir in the drained tomato flesh and the smoked salmon. Continue to cook, stirring for 3–4 minutes, or until the eggs are set to personal preference.

3 Meanwhile, place the halved tomatoes on the grill rack and grill for 2 minutes. When the egg mixture is set, use to fill the warm tomato shells. Sprinkle with snipped chives and serve two tomato cups per person.

Hot Garlic-stuffed Mushrooms

INGREDIENTS

serves 4
calories per
mushroom

94

4 large field mushrooms

4 sprays olive oil

2–3 garlic cloves, crushed

2 shallots

25 g/1 oz fresh wholemeal breadcrumbs

few fresh basil sprigs

25 g/1 oz ready-to-eat dried apricots, chopped

1 tbsp pine kernels

55 g/2 oz feta cheese

pepper

1 Preheat the oven to 180°C/350°F/Gas Mark 4. Remove the stalks from the mushrooms and set aside. Spray the bases of the mushrooms with the oil and place undersides up in a roasting tin.

2 Put the mushroom stalks in a food processor with the garlic, shallots and breadcrumbs. Reserve a few basil sprigs for the garnish then place the remainder in the food processor with the apricots, pine kernels and feta cheese. Add pepper to taste.

3 Process for 1–2 minutes, or until a stuffing consistency is formed, then divide among the mushroom caps.

4 Bake for 10–12 minutes, or until the mushrooms are tender and the stuffing is crisp on the top. Serve garnished with the reserved basil sprigs.

Courgette, Carrot & Tomato Frittata

INGREDIENTS

serves 4
calories per
portion

100

2 sprays olive oil

1 onion, cut into small wedges

1–2 garlic cloves, crushed

2 eggs

2 egg whites

1 courgette, about 85 g/3 oz, trimmed and grated

2 carrots, about 115 g/4 oz, peeled and grated

2 tomatoes, chopped

pepper

1 tbsp shredded fresh basil, for sprinkling

1 Heat the oil in a large non-stick frying pan, add the onion and garlic and sauté for 5 minutes, stirring frequently. Beat the eggs and egg whites together in a bowl then pour into the pan. Using a spatula or fork, pull the egg mixture from the sides of the pan into the centre.

2 Once the base has set lightly, add the grated courgette and carrots with the tomatoes. Add pepper to taste and continue to cook over a low heat until the eggs are set to personal preference.

3 Sprinkle with the shredded basil and cut the frittata into quarters. Serve one quarter per person.

Crisp Bread Bruschetta

serves 4
calories per
crisp bread

INGREDIENTS

4 crisp breads

2 tsp low fat herb-flavoured
cream cheese

55 g/2 oz rocket

½ small melon, such as
Ogen or Gallia

25 g/1 oz seedless grapes

2 cherry tomatoes (optional)

85 g/3 oz lean boiled ham,
thinly sliced

4 raspberries (optional)

4 thin slices peeled cucumber
(optional)

¼ small apple, thinly sliced
(optional)

pepper

1 Spread the crisp breads with the low fat
cream cheese and top with the rocket.

2 Discard the seeds and skin from the melon
and cut into tiny wedges. Arrange on top of
the rocket and arrange the grapes on top.
Sprinkle with pepper and serve. You can vary
the toppings using the cherry tomatoes, ham,
raspberries and thin slices of cucumber
and apple, for example.

Filo-wrapped Asparagus

INGREDIENTS

serves 4
calories per
portion

96

FOR THE DIP

85 g/3 oz natural cottage cheese

1 tbsp semi-skimmed milk

4 spring onions, trimmed and finely chopped

2 tbsp chopped fresh mixed herbs, such as basil, mint and tarragon

pepper

FOR THE ASPARAGUS

20 asparagus spears

5 sheets filo pastry

lemon wedges, to serve

1 Preheat the oven to 190°C/375°F/Gas Mark 5. To make the dip, put the cottage cheese in a bowl and add the milk. Beat until smooth then stir in the spring onions, chopped herbs and pepper to taste. Place in a serving bowl, cover lightly and chill in the refrigerator until required.

2 Cut off and discard the woody end of the asparagus and shave with a vegetable peeler to remove any woody parts from the spears.

3 Cut the filo pastry into quarters and place one sheet on a work surface. Brush lightly with water then place a spear at one end. Roll up to encase the spear, and place on a large baking sheet. Repeat until all the asparagus spears are wrapped in pastry.

4 Bake for 10–12 minutes, or until the pastry is golden. Serve 5 spears per person with lemon wedges and the dip (a quarter per person) on the side.

Pepper & Basil Pots

INGREDIENTS

serves 4
calories per
pot

69

1 tsp olive oil

2 shallots, finely chopped

2 garlic cloves, crushed

pepper

2 red peppers, peeled, deseeded and sliced into strips

1 orange pepper, peeled, deseeded and sliced into strips

4 tomatoes, thinly sliced

2 tbsp shredded fresh basil

salad leaves, to serve

1 Lightly brush 4 ramekin dishes with the oil. Mix the shallots and garlic together in a bowl and season with pepper to taste.

2 Layer the red and orange peppers with the tomatoes in the prepared ramekin dishes, sprinkling each layer with the shallot mixture and shredded basil. When all the ingredients have been added, cover lightly with clingfilm or baking paper. Weigh down using small weights and leave in the refrigerator for at least 6 hours, or preferably overnight.

3 When ready to serve, remove the weights and carefully run a knife around the edges. Invert onto serving plates and serve with salad leaves.

Mushroom Pâté

INGREDIENTS

serves 4
calories per
portion

61

not including
crisp breads

15 g/½ oz dried porcini
mushrooms

1 tsp olive oil

2 shallots, finely chopped

2 garlic cloves, crushed

1 fresh jalapeño chilli,
deseeded and finely chopped

2 celery sticks, trimmed and
finely chopped

225 g/8 oz closed cup
mushrooms, wiped and sliced

grated rind and juice of
1 orange

25 g/1 oz fresh breadcrumbs

1 tbsp chopped fresh parsley

1 small egg, beaten

pepper

TO SERVE
raw vegetable sticks
crisp breads

1 Preheat the oven to 180°C/350°F/Gas Mark 4.
Put the dried mushrooms in a bowl and cover
with almost boiling water. Leave to soak for
30 minutes then drain, chop and reserve.

2 Heat the oil in a medium heavy-based
saucepan, then add the shallots, garlic, chilli
and celery. Cook, stirring frequently for 3
minutes, then add both the dried and fresh
mushrooms and cook for a further 2 minutes.

3 Add the orange juice and continue to cook
for 3–4 minutes, or until the mushrooms have
collapsed. Remove the pan from the heat and
stir in the orange rind, breadcrumbs, parsley,
beaten egg and pepper to taste. Mix well.

4 Spoon the mixture into 4 individual ramekin
dishes and level the surfaces. Place the dishes
in a small baking tin and pour enough water
to come halfway up the sides of the ramekins.

5 Bake for 15–20 minutes, or until a skewer
inserted in the centre of each ramekin comes
out clean. Remove and either leave to stand
for 10 minutes before serving warm or chill
until ready to serve. Turn out and serve with
vegetable sticks and crisp breads.

Spicy Stuffed Peppers

INGREDIENTS

serves 4
calories per
pepper

93

4 assorted coloured peppers

3 sprays olive oil

1 onion, finely chopped

2 garlic cloves, chopped

2.5-cm/1-inch piece fresh root ginger, peeled and grated

1–2 fresh serrano chillies, deseeded and chopped

1 tsp ground cumin

1 tsp ground coriander

85 g/3 oz cooked brown basmati rice

1 large carrot, about 115 g/4 oz, peeled and grated

1 large courgette, about 85 g/3 oz, trimmed and grated

25 g/1 oz ready-to-eat dried apricots, finely chopped

1 tbsp chopped fresh coriander

pepper

150 ml/5 fl oz water

fresh herbs, to garnish

1 Preheat the oven to 190°C/375°F/Gas Mark 5. Cut the tops off the peppers and reserve. Discard the seeds from each pepper. Place the peppers in a large bowl and cover with boiling water. Leave to soak for 10 minutes then drain and reserve.

2 Heat a non-stick frying pan and spray with the oil. Add the onion, garlic, ginger and chillies and sauté for 3 minutes, stirring frequently. Sprinkle in the ground spices and continue to cook for a further 2 minutes.

3 Remove the pan from the heat and stir in the rice, carrot, courgette, apricots, chopped coriander, and pepper to taste. Stir well, then use to stuff the peppers.

4 Place the stuffed peppers in an ovenproof dish large enough to allow the peppers to stand upright. Put the reserved tops in position. Pour the water around their bases, cover loosely with the lid or foil and bake for 25–30 minutes, or until piping hot. Serve garnished with herbs.

Open Rösti Omelette

serves 4
calories per portion

99

INGREDIENTS

55 g/2 oz old potatoes, peeled and grated

1 onion, grated

2 garlic cloves, crushed

1 carrot, about 115 g/4 oz, peeled and grated

4 sprays olive oil

1 yellow pepper, peeled and thinly sliced

1 courgette, about 85 g/3 oz, trimmed and thinly sliced

85 g/3 oz cherry tomatoes, halved

2 eggs

3 egg whites

pepper

1 tbsp snipped fresh chives

fresh rocket, to garnish

1 Put the grated potatoes into a large bowl and cover with cold water. Leave for 15 minutes then drain, rinse thoroughly and dry on absorbent kitchen paper or a clean tea towel. Mix with the grated onion, garlic and carrot.

2 Heat a heavy-based non-stick frying pan and spray with the oil. Add the potato, onion, garlic and carrot mixture and cook over a low heat for 5 minutes, pressing the vegetables down firmly with a spatula. Add the peeled pepper and courgette slices. Cover with a lid or crumpled piece of foil and cook very gently, stirring occasionally, for 5 minutes.

3 Add the halved cherry tomatoes and cook for a further 2 minutes, or until the vegetables are tender.

4 Beat the whole eggs, egg whites, pepper to taste and the chives together in a bowl. Pour over the vegetable mixture and cook for 4–5 minutes, stirring the egg from the sides of the pan towards the centre, until the vegetables are tender and the eggs are set. Serve immediately, a quarter per person, garnished with rocket leaves.

2 Light Lunches & Snacks

Soups are a great idea for lunch or when a light snack is required, and in this chapter there are some super recipes. Try the deliciously warming Sweet Potato & Garlic Soup, or a salad – such as Spicy Warm Crab Salad or Fruity Cottage Cheese Salad – all guaranteed to please.

Herby Vegetable Soup

INGREDIENTS

serves 4
calories per
portion

98

2 sprays olive oil

1 onion, chopped

2 carrots, about 115 g/4 oz,
peeled and chopped

2 celery sticks, trimmed
and sliced

1 potato, about 55 g/2 oz,
peeled and chopped

40 g/1½ oz quick-cook pearl
barley

850 ml/1½ pints vegetable
stock

1 bouquet garni

pepper

150 ml/5 fl oz semi-skimmed
milk

1 tbsp chopped fresh mixed
herbs, such as parsley, chives
and oregano

2 tbsp low fat natural yogurt,
to serve

1 Heat a large saucepan and spray with the oil. Add the onion, carrots, celery and potato and cook over a low heat, stirring frequently, for 5 minutes. Rinse the pearl barley then add to the saucepan together with the stock and bouquet garni and pepper to taste.

2 Bring to the boil, reduce the heat to a simmer, cover with a lid and simmer for 15 minutes, or until the vegetables are tender. Discard the bouquet garni, stir in the milk and heat gently for 3 minutes. Stir in the chopped herbs and adjust the seasoning, if necessary. Divide equally between 4 warmed bowls with a spoonful of yogurt swirled round in each.

Speedy Minestrone Soup

INGREDIENTS

serves 4
calories per
portion

99

2 sprays olive oil

1 onion, finely chopped

1 large carrot, about
115 g/4 oz, peeled and diced

2 celery sticks, trimmed
and sliced

1 bouquet garni

400 g/14 oz canned chopped
tomatoes

55 g/2 oz dried soup pasta
shells or spaghetti broken into
small lengths

850 ml/1½ pints vegetable
stock

½ small cabbage, about
225 g/8 oz

pepper

1 Heat the oil in a large saucepan, add the onion, carrot and celery and sauté gently for 5 minutes, stirring frequently. Add the bouquet garni with the chopped tomatoes. Half-fill the empty tomato can with water, swirl to remove all the remaining tomatoes then pour into the pan.

2 Add the pasta with the stock and bring to the boil. Reduce the heat to a simmer and cook for 12 minutes, or until the vegetables are almost tender.

3 Discard any outer leaves and hard central core from the cabbage and shred. Wash well, then add to the saucepan with pepper to taste. Continue to cook for 5–8 minutes, or until all the vegetables are tender, but still firm to the bite. Serve divided equally between 4 warmed bowls.

Parsnip & Broccoli Soup

serves 4
calories per
portion

97

INGREDIENTS

2 sprays olive oil

1 onion, chopped

300 g/10½ oz parsnips, peeled and chopped

850 ml/1½ pints vegetable stock

300 g/10½ oz broccoli florets

pepper

55 g/2 oz fresh or frozen sweetcorn kernels

25 g/1 oz blue cheese, such as St Agur or Roquefort

1 Heat the oil in a large saucepan, add the onion and parsnips and sauté for 5 minutes, stirring frequently. Add the stock, bring to the boil, cover with a lid and reduce the heat to a simmer. Cook for 10 minutes.

2 Meanwhile, trim the broccoli, discarding any woody stalks, and cut into small florets. Use the tender parts of the stalk as well as the florets. Add to the saucepan and continue to cook for a further 5–8 minutes, or until the vegetables are tender.

3 Leave to cool slightly then pass through a food processor to form a purée and return to the pan. Season with pepper to taste and add the sweetcorn and blue cheese. Heat gently, stirring occasionally, for about 5 minutes, or until the sweetcorn is tender and the cheese has melted. Serve piping hot, divided equally between 4 warmed bowls.

Miso Fish Soup

INGREDIENTS

serves 4
calories per
portion

98

850 ml/1½ pints fish stock or vegetable stock

2.5-cm/1-inch piece fresh root ginger, peeled and grated

1 tbsp mirin or dry sherry

1 fresh bird's eye chilli, deseeded and finely sliced

1 carrot, about 85 g/3 oz, peeled and thinly sliced

55 g/2 oz daikon, peeled and cut into thin strips or ½ bunch radishes, trimmed and sliced

1 yellow pepper, deseeded and cut into thin strips

85 g/3 oz shiitake mushrooms, sliced if large

40 g/1½ oz thread egg noodles

225 g/8 oz sole fillets, skinned and cut into strips

1 tbsp miso paste

4 spring onions, trimmed and shredded

1 Pour the stock into a large saucepan and add the ginger, mirin and chilli. Bring to the boil then reduce the heat and simmer for 5 minutes.

2 Add the carrot with the daikon, pepper strips, mushrooms and noodles and simmer for a further 3 minutes.

3 Add the fish strips with the miso paste and continue to cook for 2 minutes, or until the fish is tender. Divide equally between 4 serving bowls, top with the spring onions and serve.

Sweet Potato & Garlic Soup

INGREDIENTS

serves 4
calories per portion

92

1 whole garlic bulb

2 sprays olive oil

1 onion, chopped

300 g/10½ oz sweet potatoes, peeled and chopped

1 litre/1¾ pints vegetable stock

115 g/4 oz French beans, trimmed and finely chopped

pepper

4 tbsp low fat natural yogurt

1 tbsp snipped fresh chives

1 Preheat the oven to 190°C/375°F/Gas Mark 5. Pull the garlic bulb apart and put in a small roasting tin. Roast in the oven for 20 minutes, or until soft. Remove and leave to cool before squeezing out the soft insides. Reserve.

2 Heat the oil in a heavy-based saucepan, add the onion and sweet potato and cook, stirring constantly, for 5 minutes. Add the stock and bring to the boil. Cover with a lid, reduce the heat and simmer for 10 minutes. Add the French beans and the roasted garlic flesh and continue to simmer for 10 minutes, or until the potatoes are tender. Remove and leave to cool slightly.

3 Reserve 2 tablespoons of the cooked green beans, then pass the soup through a food processor and return to the rinsed-out saucepan. Add the reserved beans with pepper to taste and heat through for 3 minutes.

4 Divide equally between 4 warmed serving bowls, swirl a spoonful of yogurt in each and sprinkle with snipped fresh chives. Serve immediately.

Warm Salmon & Mango Salad

INGREDIENTS

serves 4
calories per
portion

94

115 g/4 oz sungold or red cherry tomatoes

85 g/3 oz salmon fillets, skinned and cut into small cubes

1 large ripe mango (about 150g/5½ oz peeled fruit), peeled and cut into small chunks

2 tbsp orange juice

1 tbsp soy sauce

115 g/4 oz assorted salad leaves

½ cucumber, trimmed and sliced into batons

6 spring onions, trimmed and chopped

FOR THE DRESSING

4 tbsp low fat natural yogurt

1 tsp soy sauce

1 tbsp finely grated orange rind

1 Cut half the tomatoes in half and set aside.

2 Thread the salmon with the whole tomatoes and half the mango chunks onto 4 kebab sticks. Mix the orange juice and soy sauce together in a small bowl and brush over the kebabs. Leave to marinate for 15 minutes, brushing with the remaining orange juice mixture at least once more.

3 Arrange the salad leaves on a serving platter with the reserved halved tomatoes, mango chunks, the cucumber batons and the spring onions.

4 Preheat the grill to high and line the grill rack with foil. To make the dressing, mix the yogurt, soy sauce and grated orange rind together in a small bowl and reserve.

5 Place the salmon kebabs on the grill rack, brush again with the marinade and grill for 5–7 minutes, or until the salmon is cooked. Turn the kebabs over halfway through cooking and brush with any remaining marinade.

6 Divide the prepared salad between 4 plates, top each with a kebab, and then drizzle with the dressing.

Fruity Cottage Cheese Salad

INGREDIENTS

serves 4
calories per
portion

98

85 g/3 oz cottage cheese

1 tsp chopped fresh parsley

1 tbsp snipped fresh chives

1 tsp chopped fresh chervil
or basil

2 assorted coloured peppers,
deseeded and peeled

1 small melon, such as Ogen
(about 300 g/10½ oz after
peeling and deseeding)

175 g/6 oz assorted salad
leaves

55 g/2 oz seedless grapes

1 red onion, thinly sliced

FOR THE DRESSING

3 tbsp freshly squeezed lime
juice

1 small fresh red chilli,
deseeded and finely chopped

1 tsp clear honey

1 tbsp soy sauce

1 Place the cottage cheese in a bowl and stir in the chopped herbs. Cover lightly and reserve.

2 Cut the peeled peppers into thin strips and reserve. Cut the melon in half, discard the seeds and cut into small wedges. Remove and discard the rind, or run a sharp knife between the skin and flesh to loosen, then cut the flesh horizontally across. Push the flesh in alternate directions but so that it still sits on the skin. Reserve.

3 Arrange the salad leaves on a large serving platter with the melon wedges.

4 Spoon the herb-flavoured cottage cheese on the platter and arrange the reserved peppers, the grapes and red onion slices around the cheese.

5 To make the dressing, mix the lime juice, chilli, honey and soy sauce together in a small bowl or jug then drizzle over the salad and serve as 4 portions.

Spicy Warm Crab Salad

INGREDIENTS

serves 4
calories per
portion

96

2 sprays sunflower oil

1 fresh serrano chilli,
deseeded and finely chopped

115 g/4 oz mangetouts, cut in
half diagonally

6 spring onions, trimmed
and finely shredded

25 g/1 oz frozen sweetcorn
kernels

150 g/5½ oz white crabmeat,
drained if canned

55 g/2 oz peeled raw prawns,
thawed if frozen

1 carrot, about 85 g/3 oz,
peeled and grated

115 g/4 oz beansprouts

225 g/8 oz fresh baby
spinach leaves

1 tbsp finely grated
orange rind

2 tbsp orange juice

1 tbsp chopped fresh
coriander, for sprinkling

1 Heat a wok and when hot, spray in the oil and heat for 30 seconds. Add the chilli and mangetouts then stir-fry over a medium heat for 2 minutes.

2 Add the spring onions and sweetcorn and continue to stir-fry for a further 1 minute.

3 Add the crabmeat, prawns, grated carrot, beansprouts and spinach leaves. Stir in the orange rind and juice and stir-fry for 2–3 minutes, or until the spinach has begun to wilt and everything is cooked. Serve divided equally between 4 bowls, sprinkled with the chopped coriander.

Warm Oriental-style Salad

INGREDIENTS

serves 4
calories per
portion

98

115 g/4 oz broccoli florets

115 g/4 oz baby carrots,
scraped and cut in half
lengthways

140 g/5 oz pak choi

2 sprays sunflower oil

1 red onion, sliced

1–2 fresh bird's eye chillies,
deseeded and sliced

2.5-cm/1-inch fresh root
ginger, peeled and grated

2 whole star anise

1 red pepper, deseeded
and cut into strips

1 orange pepper, deseeded
and cut into strips

115 g/4 oz baby courgettes,
trimmed and sliced diagonally

115 g/4 oz baby sweetcorn,
sliced in half lengthways

2 tbsp orange juice

1 tbsp soy sauce

1 tbsp cashew nuts

1 Cut the broccoli into tiny florets then bring a small saucepan of water to the boil and add the halved carrots. Cook for 3 minutes then add the broccoli and cook for a further 2 minutes. Drain and plunge into cold water then drain again and reserve.

2 Arrange 25 g/1 oz of pak choi on a large serving platter. Shred the remainder and set aside.

3 Heat a wok and when hot, add the oil and heat for 30 seconds. Add the sliced onion, chillies, ginger and star anise and stir-fry for 1 minute. Add the pepper strips, courgettes and baby sweetcorn and stir-fry for a further 2 minutes.

4 Pour in the orange juice and soy sauce and continue to stir-fry for a further 1 minute before adding the reserved shredded pak choi. Stir-fry for 2 minutes, or until the vegetables are tender but still firm to the bite. Arrange the warm salad on the pak choi-lined serving platter, scatter the cashew nuts over the top and serve as 4 portions.

Mixed Cabbage Coleslaw

INGREDIENTS

serves 4
calories per
portion

96

85 g/3 oz red cabbage

85 g/3 oz hard white cabbage

55 g/2 oz green cabbage

2 carrots, about 175 g/6 oz, peeled and grated

1 white onion, finely sliced

2 red apples, cored and chopped

4 tbsp orange juice

2 celery sticks, trimmed and finely sliced

55 g/2 oz canned sweetcorn kernels

2 tbsp raisins

FOR THE DRESSING

4 tbsp low fat natural yogurt

1 tbsp chopped fresh parsley

pepper

1 Discard the outer leaves and hard central core from the cabbages and shred finely. Wash well in plenty of cold water and drain thoroughly.

2 Place the cabbages in a bowl and stir in the carrots and onion. Toss the apples in the orange juice and add to the cabbages together with any remaining orange juice, and the celery, sweetcorn and raisins. Mix well.

3 For the dressing, mix the yogurt, parsley, and pepper to taste, in a bowl then pour over the cabbage mixture. Stir and serve as 4 portions.

Fish & Mango Kebabs

INGREDIENTS

serves 4
calories per
kebab

96

85 g/3 oz fresh tuna steak

85 g/3 oz swordfish

1 courgette, cut into chunks

1 fresh ripe mango, peeled
and cut into cubes (about
115 g/4 oz peeled flesh)

2 limes, cut into wedges

2 tbsp sweet chilli sauce

4 tbsp low fat natural yogurt

1 tbsp chopped fresh coriander

TO GARNISH
fresh herbs
lime wedges

1 Preheat the grill to high and line the grill rack with foil. Discard any bones from the fish and cut into bite-sized pieces.

2 Thread the fish, courgette, mango and lime wedges onto 4 presoaked wooden skewers and brush lightly with 1 tablespoon of chilli sauce.

3 Mix the yogurt, the remaining 1 tablespoon of chilli sauce and the chopped coriander together in a bowl until smooth. Spoon into a serving dish, cover lightly and chill in the refrigerator until required.

4 Cook the kebabs under the grill for 5–7 minutes, or until the fish is cooked. Turn the kebabs at least once during cooking. Transfer to a serving plate, garnish with fresh herbs and lime wedges and serve with the dipping sauce.

Chicken Sesame Kebabs

INGREDIENTS

serves 4
calories per
2 kebabs

94

115 g/4 oz skinless, boneless chicken breast, cut into thin strips, or chicken stir-fry strips

3 tbsp lemon juice

1½ tbsp soy sauce

1 tsp clear honey

175 g/6 oz assorted salad leaves

1 red onion, thinly sliced

1 large carrot, peeled and grated

1 chicory head (optional)

bunch of radishes, trimmed, washed and sliced

1 tbsp sesame seeds

3 tbsp low fat natural yogurt

1 Thread the chicken onto 8 presoaked wooden skewers.

2 Mix 2 tablespoons of lemon juice, 1 tablespoon of soy sauce and the honey together in a small bowl. Brush the mixture over the chicken and leave to marinate for at least 15 minutes.

3 Preheat the grill to high and line the grill rack with foil. Arrange the salad leaves on a large serving platter and top with the sliced onion and grated carrot. Divide the chicory into separate leaves, if using, and place around the edge of the platter. Scatter over the radishes.

4 Cook the chicken kebabs under the grill for 8–10 minutes or until the chicken is thoroughly cooked. Remove from the grill and sprinkle with the sesame seeds.

5 Mix the yogurt, the remaining lemon juice and soy sauce together in a small bowl and drizzle over the salad. Serve 2 kebabs per portion.

Turkey & Plum Bites

INGREDIENTS

serves 4
calories per
portion

96

140 g/5 oz skinless turkey steaks, cut into bite-sized pieces

4 baby onions

2 ripe plums, stoned and cut into 4 wedges

2 tbsp plum sauce

2 tbsp orange juice

1 spray sunflower oil

1–2 fresh bird's eye chillies, deseeded and sliced

1 small yellow pepper, deseeded and cut into strips

115 g/4 oz pak choi, shredded

1 Thread the turkey onto 4 presoaked wooden skewers with the baby onions and plum wedges.

2 Mix 1 tablespoon of plum sauce and 1 tablespoon of orange juice together in a small bowl and use to brush over the turkey kebabs. Leave to marinate for at least 15 minutes, longer if time permits.

3 Preheat the grill to high and line the grill rack with foil. Cook the kebabs under the grill for 8–10 minutes, or until the turkey is thoroughly cooked. Turn the kebabs halfway through cooking.

4 Heat a wok until hot, spray with the oil and heat for 30 seconds. Add the chillies and pepper strips and stir-fry for 1–2 minutes. Add the remaining plum sauce and orange juice and stir-fry for a further 1 minute.

5 Stir in the pak choi, and stir-fry for 1–2 minutes, or until the vegetables are tender. Serve 1 kebab per person, with the vegetables.

Thai Crab Cakes

INGREDIENTS

serves 6
calories per
portion

73

300 g/10½ oz canned crabmeat, drained

1–2 fresh bird's eye chillies, deseeded and finely chopped

6 spring onions, trimmed and thinly sliced

140 g/5 oz courgettes, grated

115 g/4 oz carrot, peeled and grated

1 tbsp chopped fresh coriander

2 tbsp cornflour

2 egg whites

1 spray sunflower oil

150 ml/5 fl oz low fat natural yogurt

Tabasco sauce, to taste

2 tsp sesame seeds

lime wedges, to garnish

1 Place the crabmeat in a bowl and stir in the chillies, spring onions, grated courgette and carrot with the chopped coriander. Add the cornflour and mix well.

2 Beat the egg whites together in a separate bowl then stir into the crab mixture and mix together.

3 Heat a non-stick frying pan and lightly spray with the oil, then drop small spoonfuls of the crab mixture into the pan. Fry the crab cakes over a low heat for 3–4 minutes, pressing down with the back of a spatula. Turn over halfway through cooking. Cook the crab cakes in batches.

4 Mix the yogurt, and Tabasco sauce to taste, in a small bowl and stir in the sesame seeds. Spoon into a small bowl and use as a dipping sauce with the cooked crab cakes. Serve garnished with lime wedges, divided between 6 plates, to be sure of even-sized portions.

Potato, Leek & Feta Patties

INGREDIENTS

serves 4
calories per
portion

91

not including
tomato ketchup

1 whole garlic bulb

115 g/4 oz sweet potatoes,
peeled and cut into chunks

175 g/6 oz carrots, peeled
and chopped

115 g/4 oz leeks, trimmed
and finely chopped

55 g/2 oz feta cheese,
crumbled

1–2 tsp Tabasco sauce,
or to taste

1 tbsp chopped fresh coriander

pepper

fresh herbs or salad, to
garnish

tomato ketchup, to serve
(optional)

1 Break the garlic bulb open, place in a small roasting tin and roast for 20 minutes, or until soft. Remove and when cool enough to handle, squeeze out the roasted garlic flesh.

2 Cook the sweet potatoes and carrots in a large saucepan of boiling water for 15 minutes, or until soft. Drain and mash then mix in the roasted garlic flesh.

3 Add the leeks, feta cheese, Tabasco sauce to taste, coriander and pepper to the sweet potato mixture. Cover and leave to chill in the refrigerator for at least 30 minutes.

4 Preheat the oven to 190°C/375°F/Gas Mark 5. Using slightly dampened hands, shape the sweet potato mixture into 8 small round patties and place on a non-stick baking sheet. Bake for 15–20 minutes, or until piping hot. Garnish with fresh herbs or salad and serve with tomato ketchup, if using. Divide the patties between 4 plates, 2 patties per person, to be sure of the portions.

Stuffed Peppers

INGREDIENTS

serves 4
calories per
pepper

95

4 assorted coloured peppers

6 spring onions, trimmed and finely chopped

115 g/4 oz closed cup mushrooms, chopped

25 g/1 oz sun-dried tomatoes, chopped

1 tbsp chopped fresh mint

85 g/3 oz cooked or canned broad beans, roughly chopped

25 g/1 oz ready-to-eat dried apricots, chopped

pepper

15 g/½ oz Parmesan cheese, finely grated

salad leaves, to serve (optional)

1 Preheat the oven to 190°C/375°F/Gas Mark 5. Cut the peppers in half and discard the seeds. Place the pepper halves in a large heatproof dish and cover with boiling water. Leave to stand for 10 minutes then drain and reserve.

2 Put the spring onions, mushrooms, tomatoes, mint, broad beans, apricots and pepper to taste in a large bowl and stir well. Use to fill the halved peppers, and place in a large ovenproof dish. Sprinkle cheese over the top of each filled pepper. Pour in about 5 cm/2 inches of hot water, cover loosely with foil and cook in the oven for 25 minutes, or until the peppers are piping hot.

3 Remove and drain the peppers. Serve hot, either by themselves or with a salad.

Stuffed Courgettes

INGREDIENTS

serves 4
calories per
courgette

4 courgettes, about 175 g/6 oz each

1 spray olive oil

1 small onion, roughly chopped

2 garlic cloves, chopped

115 g/4 oz carrots, peeled and grated

115 g/4 oz canned red kidney beans, drained and rinsed

1 tbsp tomato purée (optional)

1 tbsp chopped fresh coriander

pepper

150 ml/5 fl oz water

4 tomatoes, thickly sliced

1 Preheat the oven to 190°C/375°F/Gas Mark 5. Cut the courgettes in half lengthways and scoop out the centres with a spoon. Chop the scooped out flesh and place in a food processor. Put the courgette hollows into a large heatproof dish and pour over enough boiling water to cover. Leave to stand for 10 minutes then drain and reserve.

2 Add the oil, onion, garlic, carrots, beans, tomato purée if using, and chopped coriander to the food processor and process until blended. Season the mixture with pepper, then use to stuff the hollowed-out courgettes and level the surface.

3 Place the filled courgettes in a large ovenproof dish and pour around the water. Cover loosely with foil and bake for 35 minutes.

4 Remove from the oven and place the sliced tomatoes on top. Return to the oven and continue to cook for a further 10 minutes, or until the courgettes are tender and the filling is piping hot. Serve.

Tomato Ratatouille

INGREDIENTS

serves 4
calories per
portion

92

4 sprays olive oil

1 onion, cut into small wedges

2–4 garlic cloves, chopped

1 small aubergine, trimmed
and chopped

1 small red pepper, deseeded
and chopped

1 small yellow pepper,
deseeded and chopped

1 courgette, trimmed and
chopped

2 tbsp tomato purée

3 tbsp water

115 g/4 oz mushrooms, sliced
if large

225 g/8 oz ripe tomatoes,
chopped

pepper

1 tbsp shredded fresh basil,
to garnish

25 g/1 oz Parmesan cheese,
freshly shaved, to serve

1 Heat the oil in a heavy-based saucepan,
add the onion, garlic and aubergine and cook,
stirring frequently for 3 minutes.

2 Add the peppers and courgette. Mix the
tomato purée and water together in a small
bowl and stir into the pan. Bring to the boil,
cover with a lid, reduce the heat to a simmer
and cook for 10 minutes.

3 Add the mushrooms and chopped tomatoes
with pepper to taste and continue to simmer
for 12–15 minutes, stirring occasionally, until
the vegetables are tender.

4 Divide the ratatouille between 4 warmed
bowls, garnish each with shredded basil and
serve with freshly shaved Parmesan cheese
to sprinkle over.

Thai-style Tom Yam

INGREDIENTS

serves 4
calories per
portion

97

200 g/7 oz raw prawns, peeled and deveined, heads and tails removed and reserved

1.7 litres/3 pints water

2 lemongrass stalks, bruised

3 fresh bird's eye chillies, sliced

about 1-cm/½-inch piece fresh root ginger, peeled and roughly chopped

few fresh coriander sprigs

1 large carrot, peeled and grated

85 g/3 oz French beans, trimmed and chopped

25 g/1 oz thread egg noodles

1–2 tbsp Thai fish sauce

2 tbsp lime juice

115 g/4 oz fresh or canned straw mushrooms, trimmed or drained

pepper

few fresh coriander leaves, to garnish

1 Put the reserved prawn trimmings into a large saucepan, add the water, lemongrass stalks, 2 of the chillies, the root ginger and a few coriander sprigs and bring to the boil. Reduce the heat and simmer for 30 minutes then strain, discarding the solids and reserving the fish stock.

2 Pour the fish stock into a clean saucepan and add the remaining sliced chilli with the carrot, beans and egg noodles. Bring to the boil, then reduce the heat and simmer for 5 minutes.

3 Add the fish sauce, lime juice and mushrooms together with the raw peeled prawns and cook for 3 minutes, or until the prawns are cooked and have turned pink. Add pepper if necessary, garnish with coriander leaves and serve, divided equally between 4 warmed bowls.

Warm Duck Salad

INGREDIENTS

serves 4
calories per
portion

98

175 g/6 oz duck breast,
all fat removed

2–3 sprays sunflower oil

2.5-cm/1-inch piece fresh root
ginger, peeled and grated

1 fresh serrano chilli,
deseeded and sliced

1 red onion, cut into thin
wedges

2 celery sticks, trimmed and
finely sliced

1 small red pepper, deseeded
and finely sliced

1 tbsp soy sauce

115 g/4 oz courgettes, trimmed
and sliced

2 ripe but still firm plums,
stoned and sliced

85 g/3 oz pak choi, sliced

1 tbsp chopped fresh coriander

1 Cut the duck breast into thin strips and
reserve. Heat a wok until very hot then spray
with the oil and heat for 30 seconds. Add the
ginger, chilli and duck strips and stir-fry for
1–2 minutes, or until the duck strips are
browned.

2 Add the onion wedges and celery and pepper
slices and continue to stir-fry for 3 minutes.

3 Add the soy sauce, courgettes and plums
to the wok and stir-fry for 2 minutes before
stirring in the shredded pak choi and the
chopped coriander. Stir-fry for a further minute
then serve, divided equally between 4 bowls.

3 Dinners

There are meat, fish, poultry and vegetarian ideas contained in this chapter, all of which will enable you to watch your intake of calories while at the same time not miss out on any flavour. Choose from Gingered Prawn Wraps, which are good for sharing, Beef, Pepper & Mushroom Sauté or a delicious Vegetable & Filo Pie, all of which are full of taste and crammed with health-giving nutrients.

Gingered Prawn Wraps

INGREDIENTS

serves 4
calories per
portion

99

140 g/5 oz carrots, peeled

3 celery sticks, trimmed

½ cucumber, peeled if
preferred

1 red pepper, deseeded

large lettuce leaves, such
as iceberg

1–2 sprays sunflower oil

2–4 garlic cloves, crushed

1–2 fresh red jalapeño chillies,
deseeded and chopped

2.5-cm/1-inch piece fresh root
ginger, peeled and grated

2 tsp finely grated lime rind

3 tbsp lime juice

225 g/8 oz raw king prawns,
peeled and deveined

pepper

1 Cut the carrots, celery, cucumber and red pepper into thin sticks. Place all the prepared vegetables and the lettuce leaves on a large serving platter and reserve.

2 Spray a non-stick frying pan with the oil, add the garlic, chillies and ginger and sauté for 1 minute, stirring constantly. Add the lime rind and juice and stir until well mixed.

3 Add the prawns and cook, stirring, for 3–4 minutes, or until the prawns have turned pink. Add pepper to taste then drain and place on the serving platter, to be served as 4 portions.

4 To eat, take a lettuce leaf, top with some prepared vegetables then some prawns, fold over and enjoy.

Curry-topped Salmon

serves 4
calories per
fillet

97

INGREDIENTS

4 salmon fillets, about
175 g/6 oz each

40 g/1½ oz fresh wholemeal
breadcrumbs

1½ tbsp curry paste

1 tbsp chopped fresh coriander

TO GARNISH
lemon wedges
salad leaves (optional)

1 Preheat the oven to 180°C/350°F/Gas Mark 4.
Discard any fine bones from the salmon fillets
and rinse lightly. Pat dry with kitchen paper.

2 Mix the breadcrumbs, curry paste and
chopped coriander together in a bowl until
well blended.

3 Place each salmon fillet on a sheet of foil
and pat the curry-flavoured breadcrumbs on
top of each. Cover with another sheet of foil
and place on one or two large baking sheets.

4 Bake for 10 minutes then remove the top
sheet of foil and cook for a further 10 minutes,
or until the salmon is tender. Serve garnished
with lemon wedges and salad leaves.

Sole with Oranges

INGREDIENTS

serves 4
calories per
fillet

99

4 sole fillets, about 115 g/4 oz each

2.5-cm/1-inch piece fresh root ginger, peeled and grated

2–3 garlic cloves, crushed

1 tbsp grated orange rind

4 tbsp orange juice

1 tbsp soy sauce

salad, to serve

TO GARNISH
orange wedges
fresh parsley

1 Remove any fine bones from the sole fillets and rinse lightly. Pat dry with kitchen paper and place in a large shallow dish.

2 Mix the ginger, garlic, orange rind and juice and soy sauce together in a bowl and pour over the fish. Cover loosely and leave to marinate in the refrigerator for at least 30 minutes, or longer if time permits. Spoon the marinade over the fish occasionally if marinating for longer.

3 Preheat the grill to high and line the grill rack with foil. Drain the marinade from the fish, reserving the marinade, and place the fish on the grill rack. Grill for 4–5 minutes, or until cooked. Spoon a little of the marinade over the fish while cooking.

4 Remove the fish from the grill rack, transfer to serving plates, garnish with orange wedges and parsley and serve with salad.

Salsa Sole

INGREDIENTS

serves 4
calories per
fillet

87

4 sole fillets, about 85 g/3 oz each, skinned

3 tomatoes, peeled, deseeded and finely chopped

1 fresh jalapeño chilli, deseeded and finely chopped

4 spring onions, trimmed and finely chopped

5-cm/2-inch piece cucumber, peeled and finely chopped

1 tbsp chopped fresh tarragon

85 g/3 oz cottage cheese

2 tbsp finely grated orange rind

4 tbsp water

pepper

orange wedges, to garnish

salad, to serve

1 Preheat the oven to 180°C/350°F/Gas Mark 4. Lightly rinse the sole fillets, pat dry on kitchen paper and reserve.

2 Put the tomatoes, chilli, spring onions and cucumber in a bowl and stir in the tarragon. Beat in the cottage cheese and 1 tablespoon of the orange rind and add pepper to taste.

3 Place the sole fillets skinned-side down on the work surface and spread the fillets with a little of the prepared salsa. Roll up each fillet and secure with a wooden cocktail stick or small skewer. Place in an ovenproof dish. Reserve the remaining salsa.

4 Blend the remaining orange rind with the water and pour around the fish. Cover with foil and bake for 15–20 minutes, or until the fish is cooked.

5 Remove the fish with a slotted spoon and place on individual serving plates. Garnish with orange wedges and serve with salad and the reserved salsa.

Sweet Potato & Tuna Fish Cakes

INGREDIENTS

serves 4
calories per
fish cake

99

not including
green beans

175 g/6 oz sweet potatoes,
peeled and chopped

175 g/6 oz canned tuna in
brine, drained

4 spring onions, trimmed
and chopped

1 tbsp grated lemon rind

1 tbsp chopped fresh coriander

pepper

lemon wedges, to garnish

freshly cooked green beans or
salad, to serve

1 Cook the sweet potatoes in a saucepan of boiling water for 10–12 minutes, or until tender when pierced with a fork. Drain and mash.

2 Flake the tuna then add to the mashed potatoes together with the chopped spring onions, lemon rind, chopped coriander and pepper to taste.

3 Mix the ingredients lightly together then, using slightly dampened hands, shape into 4 rounds. Place on a plate, cover loosely and leave to chill in the refrigerator for at least 30 minutes, longer if time permits.

4 Preheat the oven to 190°C/375°F/Gas Mark 5. Place the fish cakes on a large non-stick baking sheet and cook for 20 minutes, or until piping hot. Transfer to serving plates, garnish with lemon wedges and serve with freshly cooked green beans.

Seafood Stir-fry

INGREDIENTS

serves 4
calories per
portion
99

115 g/4 oz white fish, such as boneless monkfish fillet

2 sprays sunflower oil

1 fresh jalapeño chilli, deseeded and finely chopped

2.5-cm/1-inch piece fresh root ginger, peeled and grated

85 g/3 oz raw prawns, peeled and deveined

115 g/4 oz baby sweetcorn, sliced in half lengthways

115 g/4 oz mangetouts, trimmed

6 spring onions, trimmed and chopped

1 tbsp soy sauce

115 g/4 oz squid, cleaned and cut into thin slices

115 g/4 oz fresh spinach leaves

115 g/4 oz beansprouts

1 Discard any skin from the white fish, rinse lightly and pat dry on kitchen paper. Cut into small pieces.

2 Heat a wok and when hot, add the oil and heat for 10 seconds. Add the chilli and ginger and stir-fry for 1 minute then add the white fish and prawns and stir-fry for 2 minutes.

3 Add the baby sweetcorn, mangetouts, spring onions and soy sauce and continue to stir-fry for 2–3 minutes, or until the fish is just cooked and the prawns have almost turned completely pink.

4 Add the squid, spinach and beansprouts and continue to stir-fry for a further 2 minutes, or until the fish, prawns and squid are cooked. Serve immediately, divided equally between 4 warmed bowls.

Seared Scallops

INGREDIENTS

serves 4
calories per
portion

99

300 g/10½ oz fresh scallops

1 tsp sunflower oil

5-cm/2-inch piece fresh root ginger, peeled and grated

1 tbsp finely grated lime rind

1 orange pepper, deseeded and sliced

1 red onion, thinly sliced

115 g/4 oz wild mushrooms, such as chanterelle, or chestnut mushrooms

50 ml/2 fl oz lime juice

1 tsp clear honey (optional)

1 tbsp soy sauce

115 g/4 oz pak choi, shredded

1 Lightly rinse the scallops, discarding any thin black veins. Pat dry with kitchen paper and reserve.

2 Heat a wok and when hot add the oil. Add the grated ginger and cook, stirring for 1 minute.

3 Add the lime rind, pepper slices and onion and stir-fry for 3–4 minutes, or until the onion has softened.

4 Add the scallops and mushrooms to the wok and stir-fry for 2 minutes. Make sure that the scallops are turned over after 1 minute.

5 Pour in the lime juice, add the honey, if using, and the soy sauce. Stir together, then add the pak choi and continue to cook for 2–3 minutes, or until the scallops are tender. Serve immediately, divided equally between 4 warmed bowls.

Vegetable & Filo Pie

INGREDIENTS

serves 4
calories per
portion

95

175 g/6 oz carrots, peeled and chopped

140 g/5 oz broccoli, divided into small florets

115 g/4 oz broad beans

55 g/2 oz frozen or canned sweetcorn kernels

300 ml/10 fl oz vegetable stock

1 tbsp cornflour

2 tbsp water

1 tbsp chopped fresh coriander

3 sheets filo pastry

pepper

1 Preheat the oven to 190°C/375°F/Gas Mark 5. Cook the carrots in a saucepan of boiling water for 6 minutes, then add the broccoli florets with the broad beans and cook for a further 2 minutes. Stir in the sweetcorn, mix then drain thoroughly and reserve.

2 Heat the stock in another saucepan, add the vegetables and bring to boiling point. Blend the cornflour with the water in a bowl and stir the paste into the boiling liquid. Cook, stirring, until the sauce thickens. Stir in the chopped coriander and add pepper to taste. Spoon the mixture into a 1.2-litre/2-pint pie dish and leave to cool.

3 Place the filo pastry on a clean work surface and brush one sheet lightly with a little water. Put a second sheet on top. Place the filo pastry over the filling, pressing the edges over the dish to encase completely.

4 Brush the top of the pie with a little water and put the remaining sheet of pastry decoratively on top. Bake for 25 minutes, or until the top is golden brown. Serve a quarter of the pie per person.

Turkey & Aubergine Curry

INGREDIENTS

serves 4
calories per
portion

99

2 sprays sunflower oil

1 onion, chopped

2 garlic cloves, crushed

1–2 fresh serrano chillies,
deseeded and chopped

1 tsp ground cumin

1 tsp ground coriander

½ tsp turmeric

1 small aubergine, about
225 g/8 oz, trimmed and cut
into small cubes

225 g/8 oz skinless, boneless
turkey breast, cut into cubes

2 carrots, about 175 g/6 oz,
peeled and chopped

1 small red pepper, deseeded
and chopped

450 ml/16 fl oz chicken stock

1 tbsp chopped fresh
coriander, to garnish

1 Heat a large non-stick saucepan and add the oil. Add the onion, garlic and chillies and cook, stirring, for 2 minutes. Sprinkle in all of the spices and cook, stirring constantly, for a further 2 minutes.

2 Add the aubergine and turkey cubes and cook, stirring, for 5 minutes, or until the turkey is browned all over. Add the carrots and red pepper, stir, then pour in the stock. Bring to the boil, cover with a lid and simmer for 20–25 minutes, or until the turkey is tender.

3 Sprinkle with chopped coriander and serve, divided equally between 4 warmed bowls.

The Perfect Burger

INGREDIENTS

serves 4
calories per
burger

99

175 g/6 oz fresh lean beef, such as topside, minced

2 shallots, finely chopped

1 tbsp Worcestershire sauce, or to taste

pepper

2 sprays sunflower oil

2 onions, thinly sliced

4 beef tomatoes

1–2 garlic cloves, peeled

tomato ketchup, to serve (optional)

1 Put the beef mince in a bowl and add the shallots, Worcestershire sauce and pepper to taste. Mix together then, with damp hands, shape into 4 equal-sized burgers. Place the burgers on a plate, cover lightly with clingfilm and chill in the refrigerator until required.

2 Preheat the grill to high and line the grill rack with foil. Heat a non-stick frying pan, spray with the oil and add the sliced onion. Cook over a low heat for 12–15 minutes, stirring frequently until the onions are tender. Keep warm if necessary.

3 Cut the tomatoes into thick slices and the garlic cloves into slivers. Stud the tomatoes with the garlic and place on the grill rack together with the burgers.

4 Cook the burgers for 3–4 minutes on each side, or according to personal preference. If the tomatoes are cooking too quickly, either remove them and add a little later or remove and keep warm.

5 Serve each burger between the thick tomato slices with the onion garnish, and ketchup if using.

Seared Duck with Red Onion Relish

INGREDIENTS

serves 4
calories per
duck breast

98

200 g/7 oz duck breast (after all fat and skin is removed)

1 tbsp orange rind

315 ml/10½ fl oz water

2 tbsp balsamic vinegar or red wine vinegar

2 sprays sunflower oil

2 red onions, very thinly sliced

2 garlic cloves, crushed

1 tsp dark brown sugar

1 tsp cornflour

bitter salad leaves, to serve

TO GARNISH
1 tbsp chopped fresh parsley
orange wedges

1 Lightly rinse the duck breast, pat dry with kitchen paper, slice thinly and put in a non-metallic dish that will not react with acid.

2 Blend the orange rind with 150 ml/5 fl oz water and 1 tablespoon of vinegar in a bowl and pour over the duck. Cover lightly with clingfilm and leave to marinate for at least 20 minutes. Stir occasionally during marinating.

3 Meanwhile, heat a non-stick saucepan and spray with the oil. Add the onion and garlic and cook, stirring, for 5 minutes. Sprinkle in the sugar, then add 150 ml/5 fl oz water and the vinegar. Cover with a lid and cook for 10 minutes until the onions are soft. Keep warm.

4 Heat a non-stick heavy-based frying pan, add the duck breasts with the marinade and cook gently for 6 minutes. Add the cooked onions with any liquor and stir together lightly.

5 Blend the cornflour with 1 tablespoon of water and stir into the pan. Cook, stirring, until the liquid has thickened, then cook for a further 2 minutes, or until the duck is tender and the onions are hot. Garnish with parsley and orange wedges and serve with salad.

Vegetable Chilli

INGREDIENTS

serves 4
calories per
portion

not including
pumpkin mash

2–3 sprays olive oil

1 onion, chopped

1–2 fresh serrano chillies,
deseeded and chopped

2–3 garlic cloves, chopped

2 celery sticks, trimmed
and sliced

175 g/6 oz carrots, peeled
and chopped

200 g/7 oz canned chopped
tomatoes

150 ml/5 fl oz water

1 tbsp tomato purée

115 g/4 oz canned red kidney
beans, drained and rinsed

115 g/4 oz green beans,
trimmed and chopped

pepper

1 tbsp chopped fresh coriander

freshly cooked mashed
pumpkin, to serve (optional)

1 Heat a large saucepan, spray with the oil
and add the onion, chillies and garlic. Cook
over a low heat, stirring constantly for
5 minutes. Add the celery, carrots and chopped
tomatoes. Pour the water into the empty
tomato can, swirl around, then pour it into the
saucepan. Add the tomato purée and bring to
the boil.

2 Reduce the heat to a gentle simmer then
cover with a lid and simmer for 10 minutes.
Add the red kidney beans together with the
green beans and continue to simmer for a
further 10 minutes, or until the vegetables
are tender.

3 Season with pepper to taste and add the
chopped coriander. Serve divided equally
between 4 warmed bowls, with pumpkin
mash, if using.

Roasted Vegetables

INGREDIENTS

serves 4
calories per
portion

99

1 onion, cut into wedges

2–4 garlic cloves, left whole but peeled

1 aubergine, about 225 g/8 oz, trimmed and cut into cubes

2 courgettes, about 175 g/6 oz, trimmed and cut into chunks

300 g/10½ oz butternut squash, peeled, deseeded and cut into small wedges

2 assorted coloured peppers, deseeded and cut into chunks

2 tsp olive oil

pepper

1 tbsp shredded fresh basil

1 Preheat the oven to 200°C/400°F/Gas Mark 6. Place the onion wedges, whole garlic and aubergine cubes in a large roasting tin.

2 Add the courgettes, squash and peppers to the roasting tin then pour over the oil. Turn the vegetables until they are lightly coated in the oil.

3 Roast the vegetables for 35–40 minutes, or until softened but not mushy. Turn the vegetables over occasionally during cooking.

4 Remove the vegetables from the oven, season with pepper to taste and stir. Scatter with shredded basil and serve divided between 4 warmed bowls while still warm.

Roasted Butternut Squash

INGREDIENTS

serves 4
calories per
portion

97

1 butternut squash, about 450 g/1 lb

1 onion, chopped

2–3 garlic cloves, crushed

4 small tomatoes, chopped

85 g/3 oz chestnut mushrooms, chopped

85 g/3 oz canned butter beans, drained, rinsed and roughly chopped

1 courgette, about 115 g/4 oz, trimmed and grated

1 tbsp chopped fresh oregano, plus extra to garnish

pepper

2 tbsp tomato purée

300 ml/10 fl oz water

4 spring onions, trimmed and chopped

1 tbsp Worcestershire or Hot Pepper sauce, or to taste

1 Preheat the oven to 190°C/375°F/Gas Mark 5. Prick the squash all over with a metal skewer then roast for 40 minutes, or until tender. Remove from the oven and leave until cool enough to handle.

2 Cut the squash in half, scoop out and discard the seeds then scoop out some of the flesh, making hollows in both halves. Chop the cooked flesh and put in a bowl. Place the two halves side by side in a large roasting tin.

3 Add the onion, garlic, chopped tomatoes and mushrooms to the cooked squash flesh. Add the roughly chopped butter beans, grated courgette, chopped oregano and pepper to taste and mix well. Spoon the filling into the 2 halves of the squash, packing it down as firmly as possible.

4 Mix the tomato purée with the water, spring onions and Worcestershire sauce in a small bowl and pour around the squash.

5 Cover loosely with a large sheet of foil and bake for 30 minutes, or until piping hot. Serve, divided equally between 4 warmed bowls, garnished with extra chopped oregano.

Beef, Pepper & Mushroom Sauté

INGREDIENTS

serves 4
calories per
portion

99

2 sprays olive oil

175 g/6 oz beef steak, such as topside (fat or gristle removed), cut into thin strips

2 shallots, cut into small wedges

1–2 garlic cloves, chopped

2 assorted coloured peppers, deseeded and cut into thin strips

175 g/6 oz large field mushrooms, sliced

150 ml/5 fl oz beef stock

1–2 tsp redcurrant jelly (optional)

1 tbsp chopped fresh parsley

1 Heat a non-stick frying pan, spray with oil and heat for 30 seconds. Add the steak strips and stir-fry for 1 minute, or until browned. Remove from the pan and reserve.

2 Add the shallots, garlic and peppers to the pan and cook, stirring, for 2 minutes. Add the mushrooms, stir well, pour in the stock and add the redcurrant jelly, if using. Bring to the boil, reduce the heat to a simmer and cook for 4 minutes.

3 Return the beef steak strips to the pan and cook for a further 2–4 minutes, or until the steak and vegetables are cooked to your taste. Sprinkle with the parsley and serve, divided equally between 4 warmed bowls.

98

Turkey & Apricot Tagine

INGREDIENTS

2 sprays olive oil

225 g/8 oz turkey breast steaks,
cut into bite-sized pieces

1 onion, chopped

2–3 garlic cloves, chopped

1 small aubergine, about
225 g/8 oz

1 tsp ground cinnamon

1 tsp ground cumin

1 tsp ground coriander

few saffron strands

450 ml/16 fl oz chicken stock

55 g/2 oz ready-to-eat dried
apricots, chopped

pepper

1 tbsp chopped fresh coriander

1 Heat a non-stick saucepan and spray with the oil. Then add the turkey pieces and cook for 2–3 minutes, or until browned. Remove from the pan with a slotted spoon and reserve.

2 Add the onion, garlic and aubergine to the saucepan and cook, stirring, for 5 minutes, or until the onion is beginning to soften. Sprinkle in all the spices including the saffron and cook, stirring, for 3 minutes. Pour in the stock, bring to the boil then reduce the heat to a simmer.

3 Return the turkey to the saucepan. Cover with a lid and cook for 15 minutes. Add the dried apricots to the pan and season with pepper to taste. Continue to simmer for 10 minutes, or until the turkey is tender. Sprinkle with chopped coriander and serve, divided equally between 4 warmed bowls.

Barbecued Chicken

INGREDIENTS

serves 4
calories per
drumstick

99

4 chicken drumsticks, about
100 g/3½ oz each, skinned

1 tbsp chopped fresh parsley

lemon wedges

salad, to serve

FOR THE SAUCE

1 shallot, finely chopped

1 garlic clove, crushed

1 tbsp tomato purée blended
with 150 ml/5 fl oz water

2 tbsp red wine vinegar

1 tbsp prepared mustard

1 tbsp Worcestershire sauce

1 To make the sauce, place the shallot, garlic, tomato purée mixture, red wine vinegar, mustard and Worcestershire sauce in a screw-top jar, cover with the lid and shake vigorously until well blended.

2 Rinse the chicken drumsticks and pat dry with kitchen paper. Place the drumsticks in a large ovenproof dish, pour over the sauce and leave to stand for at least 2 hours, occasionally spooning the sauce over the chicken.

3 Preheat the oven to 190°C/375°F/Gas Mark 5. Cook the chicken drumsticks in the oven for 20–25 minutes, or until thoroughly cooked. Spoon the sauce over the chicken or turn the chicken over during cooking.

4 Transfer to a serving plate, sprinkle with chopped parsley, garnish with lemon wedges and serve with salad.

Mushroom-stuffed Turkey

serves 4
calories per
escalope

98

INGREDIENTS

4 turkey escalopes, about 85 g/3 oz each

4 spring onions, trimmed and finely chopped

1–2 garlic cloves, chopped

85 g/3 oz closed cup mushrooms

1 tomato, deseeded

pepper

fresh basil sprigs or salad leaves, to garnish

1 Preheat the oven to 190°C/375°F/Gas Mark 5. Place the turkey escalopes between two sheets of baking paper and pound lightly with a meat mallet or rolling pin until about 5 mm/ ¼ inch thick. Take care not to tear the flesh. Keep covered and set aside.

2 Place the spring onions, garlic, mushrooms, tomato and pepper to taste in a food processor and process for 1 minute, or until finely chopped.

3 Divide the stuffing into 4 portions and use to spread over the turkey escalopes. Roll up the escalopes to encase the stuffing and secure with either string or wooden cocktail sticks. Cut out four 15-cm/6-inch squares of baking paper and wrap each turkey escalope in a square of paper.

4 Place the parcels in a roasting tin and bake for 20–25 minutes, or until the turkey is thoroughly cooked. Remove and serve sliced with a garnish of basil sprigs or salad leaves.

Chinese Lemon Chicken

INGREDIENTS

serves 4
calories per
portion

96

300 g/10½ oz skinless,
boneless chicken breast

chopped fresh herbs,
to garnish

FOR THE MARINADE

150 ml/5 fl oz freshly squeezed
lemon juice

1 tbsp light soy sauce

1 tbsp cornflour

1 Lightly rinse the chicken and pat dry with kitchen paper. Cut into bite-sized cubes and place in a shallow dish.

2 Mix the lemon juice and soy sauce together in a bowl. Put the cornflour in another bowl and stir in the lemon and soy mixture to form a paste. Spread over the chicken and leave to marinate for 15 minutes.

3 Heat a non-stick frying pan and add the chicken and marinade. Cook, stirring, for 10–12 minutes, or until the chicken is thoroughly cooked. Transfer to 4 serving plates, pour over the sauce and serve, garnished with fresh herbs.

Beef Stir-fry

INGREDIENTS

serves 4
calories per
portion

99

2–3 sprays olive oil

140 g/5 oz beef steak, such
as topside (fat removed), cut
into thin strips

1 orange pepper, deseeded
and cut into thin strips

4 spring onions, trimmed
and chopped

1–2 fresh jalapeño chillies,
deseeded and chopped

2–3 garlic cloves, chopped

115 g/4 oz mangetouts,
trimmed and cut in half
diagonally

115 g/4 oz large field
mushrooms, sliced

1–2 tsp hoisin sauce,
or to taste

1 tbsp orange juice

85 g/3 oz rocket or
watercress

1 Heat a wok then spray in the oil and heat
for 30 seconds. Add the beef and stir-fry for
1 minute or until browned. Using a slotted
spoon, remove and reserve.

2 Add the pepper, spring onions, chillies
and garlic and stir-fry for 2 minutes. Add the
mangetouts and mushrooms and stir-fry for a
further 2 minutes.

3 Return the beef to the wok and add the
hoisin sauce and orange juice. Stir-fry for
2–3 minutes, or until the beef is tender and the
vegetables are tender but still firm to the bite.
Stir in the rocket and stir-fry until it starts to
wilt. Serve immediately, divided equally
between 4 warmed bowls.

4 Desserts

Watching your calorie intake does not necessarily mean missing out on the sweeter things of life. Fruit, which is one of the 'superfoods' and essential for a healthy diet, provides the basis for most of the recipes featured in this chapter. Try the Fruity Stuffed Nectarines, a spoonful or two of Strawberry & Balsamic Vinegar Semifreddo to cool you down, or when you're feeling like spoiling yourself, a very thin slice of Chocolate Swiss Roll.

Fruity Stuffed Nectarines

serves 4
calories per
nectarine

84

INGREDIENTS

4 ripe but firm nectarines
or peaches

140 g/5 oz blueberries

115 g/4 oz fresh raspberries

150 ml/5 fl oz freshly squeezed
orange juice

1–2 tsp clear honey, or to taste

1 tbsp brandy (optional)

200 ml/7 fl oz low fat Greek-
style yogurt

1 tbsp finely grated orange
rind

1 Preheat the oven to 180°C/350°F/Gas Mark 4. Cut the nectarines in half, remove the stones then place in a shallow ovenproof dish.

2 Mix the blueberries and raspberries together in a bowl and use to fill the hollows left by the removal of the nectarine stones. Spoon any extra berries around.

3 Mix together the orange juice and honey, and brandy if using, in a small bowl and pour over the fruit. Blend the yogurt with the grated orange rind in another bowl and leave to chill in the refrigerator until required.

4 Bake the berry-filled nectarines for 10 minutes, or until the fruit is hot. Serve with the orange-flavoured yogurt.

Aromatic Pears

INGREDIENTS

serves 4
calories per
pear

90

4 ripe but firm pears, about
140 g/5 oz each

2 tbsp lemon juice

1 tbsp clear honey, or to taste

1 fresh jalapeño chilli,
deseeded

2 whole star anise

1 cinnamon stick, bruised

1 lemongrass stalk, bruised

1-cm/½-inch piece fresh root
ginger, peeled and sliced

2 whole cloves

4 fresh bay leaves

300 ml/10 fl oz water

1 Using a vegetable peeler, peel the pears as
thinly as possible and leave the stalk intact. If
necessary, cut off a thin slice from the base of
each pear so it will stand upright. Place in a
large bowl and pour over the lemon juice with
enough water to cover the pears.

2 Pour the honey into a large saucepan with a
lid. Add the chilli, star anise, cinnamon stick,
lemongrass stalk, ginger, cloves, bay leaves
and the water. Bring to the boil, then reduce
the heat and simmer, stirring occasionally for
5 minutes, or until the honey has dissolved.

3 Drain the pears and place in the saucepan.
Bring to almost boiling point then reduce the
heat to a gentle simmer and cover with the lid.

4 Cook for 15–20 minutes, or until the pears
are tender. Remove the pan from the heat and
leave the pears to cool in the syrup. When
cool, remove from the pan with a slotted
spoon and place in a serving dish.

5 Return the syrup to the heat and bring to
the boil. Boil for 5–8 minutes, or until reduced
by half and the syrup has thickened. Leave to
cool for 5–10 minutes then pour over the pears
and serve.

Apricot Granita

INGREDIENTS

serves 4
calories per
glass

97

450 g/1 lb fresh apricots

1 tbsp clear honey, or to taste

300 ml/10 fl oz water

2 ripe passion fruit, about
55 g/2 oz each or 2 whole star
anise and 5 cardamom pods,
bruised

4 redcurrants, to decorate

2 raspberries, halved, to
decorate (optional)

2 strawberries, halved, to
decorate (optional)

2 seedless grapes, halved, to
decorate (optional)

1 Set the freezer to rapid freeze at least 2 hours before making the granita. Cut the apricots in half, discard the stones and reserve.

2 Pour the honey into a saucepan and add the water. Scoop out the seeds and juice from the passion fruit and add these, or the spices, to the pan. Bring to the boil then reduce the heat to a simmer and cook gently for 5 minutes.

3 Add the halved apricots to the pan, cover with a lid and simmer for 10–12 minutes, or until tender. Remove from the heat and leave to cool.

4 Drain the apricots (discard the spices if used), reserve the juice, then transfer the apricots to a food processor and process for 1–2 minutes to form a purée, slowly adding a little of the juice to slacken if necessary.

5 Pour the purée into a freezerproof container and place in the freezer for 2–2½ hours, or until semi-frozen. Stir at least twice during the freezing time to break up the ice particles forming around the edges.

6 Once semi-frozen, serve spoonfuls in tall dessert glasses decorated with redcurrants, and berries and grapes if using. Remember to return the freezer to its original setting afterwards.

Fruity Yogurt Cups

serves 4
calories per
cup

63

INGREDIENTS

450 ml/16 fl oz low fat natural yogurt

1½ tbsp finely grated orange rind

225 g/8 oz mixed berries, such as blueberries, raspberries and strawberries, plus extra to decorate

fresh mint sprigs, to decorate (optional)

1 Set the freezer to rapid freeze at least 2 hours before freezing this dish. Line a 12-hole bun tin with 12 paper cake cases, or use small ramekin dishes placed on a baking tray.

2 Mix the yogurt and orange rind together in a large bowl. Cut any large strawberries into pieces so that they are the same size as the blueberries and raspberries.

3 Add the fruit to the yogurt then spoon into the paper cases or ramekins. Freeze for 2 hours, or until just frozen. Decorate with extra fruit and mint sprigs, if using, and serve. Remember to return the freezer to its original setting afterwards.

Strawberry & Balsamic Vinegar Semifreddo

serves 4
calories per glass

65

INGREDIENTS

1 tsp clear honey

85 ml/3 fl oz water

450 g/1 lb ripe strawberries, hulled

2 tbsp balsamic vinegar

4 baby strawberries or wild, halved, to decorate (optional)

fresh mint sprigs, to decorate (optional)

1 Set the freezer to rapid freeze at least 2 hours before freezing. Pour the honey and water into a saucepan and bring to the boil, stirring occasionally. Reduce the heat to a simmer then add the strawberries and simmer for 2 minutes. Remove from the heat and leave to cool.

2 Place the strawberries and syrup in a food processor with the balsamic vinegar and process for 30 seconds, or until a chunky mixture is formed.

3 Pour the mixture into a freezerproof container and freeze for 1–1½ hours, or until semi-frozen. Stir at least once during freezing. Scoop spoonfuls of the semifreddo into glasses, and serve decorated with baby or wild strawberries, and mint sprigs, if using. Remember to return the freezer to its original setting afterwards.

Apple & Mango Jelly

INGREDIENTS

serves 8
calories per
portion
59

450 ml/16 fl oz clear apple juice

1 tbsp clear honey

3 tsp powdered gelatine

1 large ripe mango, peeled and chopped into small pieces

300 g/10½ oz fresh blueberries or raspberries

1 Fill a 1.2-litre/2-pint mould or loaf tin with cold water and set aside. Pour the apple juice into a saucepan and add the honey. Place over a low heat and sprinkle in the gelatine. Bring to the boil, whisking constantly, then remove and leave to cool for at least 5 minutes.

2 Drain the mould or loaf tin and place a layer of mango and blueberries in the base. Pour in enough of the cooled apple jelly to cover then leave in the refrigerator until set. Repeat the layers until all the fruits and jelly are used.

3 Leave to set in the refrigerator for 2 hours then cover the top with clingfilm and weigh down with a few weights or clean cans. Leave to chill overnight.

4 The next day, dip the base into boiling water for about 30 seconds. Invert onto a serving platter and carefully remove the container. Serve, divided equally between 8 plates.

Ruby Fruits with Baby Meringues

INGREDIENTS

serves 4
calories per
portion

98

FOR THE MERINGUES

1 egg white

40 g/1½ oz caster sugar

FOR THE FRUIT

225 g/8 oz fresh or frozen raspberries

2 tsp clear honey

200 ml/7 fl oz water

350 g/12 oz mixed fresh fruits, such as raspberries, strawberries, blackcurrants and stoned cherries

few fresh mint sprigs, to garnish

1 Preheat the oven to 120°C/250°F/Gas Mark ½ and line a baking sheet with baking paper.

2 Whisk the egg white in a grease-free bowl until stiff then gradually add the sugar a spoonful at a time, whisking well after each addition. When all the sugar has been added and the mixture is stiff, spoon into a piping bag fitted with a large star nozzle and pipe small whirls onto the lined baking sheet. Alternatively, shape the mounds with 2 teaspoons.

3 Bake in the oven for 1 hour, or until crisp. Leave to cool before removing from the baking sheet. Store in an airtight tin.

4 Place the raspberries in a saucepan with the honey and water. Bring to the boil then reduce the heat to a simmer and cook for 5–8 minutes, or until the raspberries have collapsed. Leave to cool for 5 minutes. Transfer to a food processor and process to form a purée.

5 Press the purée through a fine sieve, adding a little extra water if the purée is too thick.

6 Prepare the fresh fruits and stir into the fruit purée. Stir until lightly coated and serve as 4 portions with the baby meringues.

Stewed Creamy Apple

INGREDIENTS

serves 4
calories per
portion

96

450 g/1 lb cooking apples,
peeled, cored and chopped

1 tbsp clear honey, or to taste

1 tsp ground cinnamon

2–3 tbsp water

300 ml/10 fl oz low fat
Greek-style yogurt

140 g/5 oz fresh raspberries

few fresh mint sprigs, to
garnish

1 Place the apples in a saucepan with the honey, cinnamon and water then place over a low heat. Cook, stirring occasionally, for 12–15 minutes, or until the apples are soft and fluffy. Remove from the heat and beat until free from any lumps. Leave to cool.

2 Place the yogurt in a large bowl and stir in the apples. Reserve a few fresh raspberries for decoration then stir the remainder gently into the apple mixture. Spoon into 4 individual dishes and chill for at least 1 hour.

3 Decorate with the reserved raspberries and the mint sprigs and serve.

Orange Cups

INGREDIENTS

serves 4
calories per
portion

98

4 large oranges

240 ml/8½ fl oz buttermilk
or low fat natural yogurt

1 tsp clear honey

1 tsp chocolate shavings
(optional)

1 Set the freezer to rapid freeze at least
2 hours before freezing. To ensure that the
oranges stand upright, cut a thin slice from
the base of each. Cut a lid from each orange at
the other end and reserve. Carefully cut down
the inside of each orange and remove the pith
and flesh from each. Do this over a bowl to
catch all the juice.

2 Discard the pith from the scooped out flesh,
then chop the flesh to make a chunky purée.
Place in a bowl with the juice. Stir in the
buttermilk and the honey, and pour into a
freezerproof container. Freeze for 1 hour. Place
the empty orange shells upside down on
kitchen paper and leave to drain.

3 Remove the orange mixture from the freezer
and stir well, breaking up any ice crystals.
Return to the freezer for a further 30 minutes,
or until semi-frozen.

4 Stir again and use to fill the orange shells.
Stand the filled oranges upright in a container.
Freeze for a further hour, or until frozen.

5 Before serving, transfer to the refrigerator
for 30 minutes to soften slightly. Serve
decorated with chocolate shavings, if using.

Summer Pavlova

INGREDIENTS

serves 6
calories per
portion

73

FOR THE MERINGUES

2 egg whites

40 g/1½ oz caster sugar

1 tsp cornflour

1 tsp vanilla extract

1 tsp vinegar

FOR THE FILLING

300 ml/10½ fl oz low fat cream cheese

150 ml/5 fl oz low fat natural yogurt

½–1 tsp vanilla extract, or to taste

300 g/10½ oz mixed berries

1 Preheat the oven to 120°C/250°F/Gas Mark ½ and line a baking sheet with non-stick baking paper. Whisk the egg whites in a grease-free bowl until stiff then gradually add the sugar a spoonful at a time, whisking well after each addition. Stir in the cornflour, vanilla extract and the vinegar.

2 When all the sugar has been added and the mixture is stiff, spoon onto the lined baking sheet and form into a 15-cm/6-inch round, hollowing out the centre to form a case.

3 Bake in the oven for 1½–2 hours, or until crisp. Switch the oven off and leave to cool in the oven. Remove from the oven and leave until cold before removing from the baking sheet. Store in an airtight container until required.

4 Beat the cream cheese and yogurt together in a bowl until well blended, then stir in the vanilla extract. Clean the fruits if necessary, cutting any large fruits into bite-sized pieces. When ready to serve, pile the cheese filling in the centre of the pavlova case, top with the fruits and serve cut into 6 slices.

Baked Apples

INGREDIENTS

serves 4
calories per
apple

78

4 cooking apples, about
225 g/8 oz each

85 g/3 oz blueberries

2 tbsp maple syrup, or to taste

6 tbsp water

low fat Greek-style yogurt,
to serve

1 Preheat the oven to 200°C/400°F/Gas Mark 6.
Using an apple corer or small, sharp-pointed
knife, remove the central core. Make a thin
slit around the centre of each apple skin.
If necessary, cut off a thin slice from the
base of each apple to ensure that the apples
stand upright. Place the apples in a large
ovenproof dish.

2 Fill the centre of each apple with the
blueberries and pour the maple syrup over
the apples. Add the water to the dish and bake
for 45 minutes–1 hour, or until the flesh feels
tender when pierced lightly with a knife.

3 Remove from the oven and serve with low fat
Greek-style yogurt.

Flapjack Buns

makes 12
calories per
bun

INGREDIENTS

175 g/6 oz porridge oats

55 g/2 oz light brown sugar

55 g/2 oz ready-to-eat dried
apricots, chopped

25 g/1 oz dried cranberries

2 tbsp flaked almonds

1 tsp ground cinnamon

2 egg whites

1 Preheat the oven to 190°C/375°F/Gas Mark 5.
Line a 12-hole bun tin with 12 paper cases.
Place the oats in a mixing bowl and add the
sugar, apricots, cranberries, almonds and
cinnamon.

2 Beat the egg whites in another bowl until
frothy, then stir into the dry ingredients and
mix well together. Using your hands, take about
1 tablespoon of the mixture and press together.
Place in a paper case. Continue until all the
mixture has been used up.

3 Bake for 15–20 minutes, or until the tops are
beginning to crisp. Remove from the oven and
leave until cold before serving.

Chocolate Swiss Roll

INGREDIENTS

serves 12
calories per
slice

92

3 eggs

70 g/2½ oz caster sugar,
plus extra for sprinkling

1 tbsp cocoa powder

115 g/4 oz self-raising flour

1 tbsp boiled water, cooled

FOR THE FILLING

225 g/8 oz cottage cheese or
low fat cream cheese

1 tbsp finely grated orange
rind

2 tsp clear honey

1 Preheat the oven to 220°C/425°F/Gas Mark 7.
Line a 30 x 23-cm/12 x 9-inch Swiss roll tin with
non-stick baking paper.

2 Break the eggs into a heatproof bowl and
add the sugar. Place the bowl over a saucepan
of simmering water and whisk until the whisk
leaves a trail when dragged across the surface.
Remove from the heat and whisk until cool.

3 Sift the cocoa powder and flour together in a
separate bowl, then stir very lightly into the
egg mixture. Add the cooled boiled water, stir
lightly then pour into the prepared tin. Tap the
tin lightly on the work surface to remove any
air bubbles.

4 Bake for 8–10 minutes, or until the top
springs back lightly when touched. Remove
from the oven. Invert the cake onto baking
paper, sprinkled with caster sugar. Remove the
tin and carefully strip off the baking paper.
Place a further sheet of baking paper on top
then carefully roll up and leave until cold.

5 To make the filling, beat the cheese, orange
rind and honey together in a bowl. When the
Swiss roll is cold unroll and spread with the
cottage cheese mixture, then carefully roll up.
Trim the edges and serve cut into thin slices.

Fresh Fruit Wedges

serves 10
calories per
wedge

99

INGREDIENTS

sunflower oil, for oiling

2 eggs

55 g/2 oz caster sugar

1 tbsp finely grated lemon rind

85 g/3 oz self-raising flour, sifted

1 tbsp freshly squeezed lemon juice, strained

FOR THE FILLING AND DECORATION

350 g/12 oz ripe plums or other fruits of your choice

225 ml/8 fl oz low fat natural set yogurt

1 tsp icing sugar, sifted

1 Preheat the oven to 220°C/425°F/Gas Mark 7. Lightly oil and base line a 23-cm/9-inch cake tin with non-stick baking paper.

2 Break the eggs into a heatproof bowl and add the caster sugar and lemon rind. Place the bowl over a saucepan of gently simmering water and whisk until the whisk leaves a trail when it is dragged lightly across the surface. Remove from the heat and whisk until cool.

3 Add the flour to the bowl and stir very lightly into the whisked mixture, taking care not to overmix. Add the lemon juice and stir lightly then pour into the prepared tin. Tap lightly on the work surface to remove any air bubbles.

4 Bake for 8–10 minutes, or until the top springs back lightly when touched. Remove from the oven and leave to cool for 10 minutes before turning out, discarding the lining paper.

5 Halve the plums, discard the stones and slice.

6 Place the sponge cake on a serving plate and spoon the yogurt on top. Arrange the plums over. Sprinkle with the sifted icing sugar and serve cut into 10 wedges.

Fruity Filo Baskets

serves 6
calories per
basket

81

INGREDIENTS

4 sheets filo pastry

300 g/10½ oz cooking apples,
peeled, cored and chopped

1 tbsp finely grated orange
rind

1 tbsp maple syrup, or to taste

2 tbsp water

3 fresh mandarins, peeled
and segmented

2 tbsp toasted flaked almonds
or flaked coconut

1 Preheat the oven to 190°C/375°F/Gas Mark 5.
Place a sheet of pastry on a clean work
surface and cut into 6 squares. Brush one
piece lightly with water and place a second
sheet on top. Brush again and repeat the
layering using another 3 pieces. Keep the
pastry moist while doing this by covering with
a clean damp cloth. Make 5 more layered filo
piles in the same way.

2 Mould the 6 filo pastry piles into 10-cm/
4-inch ovenproof containers, such as muffin
tins. Push the pastry carefully into the bases
to form baskets. Crumple a small sheet of foil
into each to help keep their shape.

3 Bake for 8–10 minutes, or until crisp. Remove
the foil and, if the bases are not crisp, return to
the oven for a further 3–5 minutes. Remove
from the oven and leave until cold.

4 Place the apples in a saucepan with the
orange rind and maple syrup. Add the water,
then cook over a low heat for 8–10 minutes or
until tender. Leave to cool slightly then beat
until smooth. Leave until cold.

5 When ready to serve, spoon the prepared
apple filling into the filo baskets and top with
the mandarin segments. Sprinkle with the
almonds flaked and serve.

5 Drinks

This chapter has something for everyone, from fruit smoothies, such as Peach or Apple & Raspberry to a refreshing glass of Fresh Lemonade. There is also a banana milkshake and even alcoholic drinks like the Summer Punch to help you relax and unwind at the end of a busy day.

Peach Smoothie

INGREDIENTS

serves 1
calories per
glass

98

1 ripe peach, about 115 g/4 oz

1 ripe passion fruit or
mandarin

2 tbsp freshly squeezed
orange juice

3 tbsp low fat natural yogurt

1 tsp clear honey (optional)

crushed ice

1 Cut the peach in half, discard the stone and slice the flesh. Reserve 1–2 slices for decoration and place the rest in a smoothie machine or blender.

2 Scoop out the seeds from the passion fruit, if using, and add to the peach slices. If using a mandarin, peel and divide into segments and add to the peach. Switch on and, with the motor running, slowly pour in the orange juice and the yogurt. Add honey to taste, if using, and blend for 30 seconds, or until smooth.

3 Half-fill a tumbler with crushed ice and pour the smoothie over. Decorate with the reserved peach slice and serve immediately.

Carrot & Broccoli Juice

INGREDIENTS

serves 1
calories per
glass

89

1 carrot, about 55 g/2 oz, peeled and cut into small chunks

about 4 tbsp water

25 g/1 oz fresh tender broccoli florets

1 large orange, peeled and divided into segments

Worcestershire sauce, to taste

crushed ice

1 celery stick

orange slice, to decorate

1 With the motor running in a smoothie machine or blender, drop in the carrot then pour in about 2 tablespoons of the water. Add the broccoli and another 2 tablespoons of water, then add the orange segments.

2 Add a few dashes of Worcestershire sauce and blend until smooth. Put some crushed ice into a tumbler and pour over the juice. Add a celery stick for stirring, then decorate with an orange slice and serve.

Spicy Tomato & Orange Smoothie

INGREDIENTS

serves 1
calories per
glass

83

115 g/4 oz ripe tomatoes
(peeled if preferred),
roughly chopped

2 spring onions, trimmed
and chopped

150 ml/5 fl oz orange juice

Tabasco sauce, to taste

crushed ice

chilled mineral water
(optional)

fresh basil sprig, to decorate

1 Put the tomatoes in a smoothie machine or
blender. Switch on and with the motor running
add the spring onions and the orange juice.

2 Add a few dashes of Tabasco sauce and
continue to blend for 1 minute, or until smooth.

3 Half-fill a tumbler with crushed ice then pour
over the juice. Top up with some chilled mineral
water, if liked, then decorate with a basil sprig
and serve.

Apple & Raspberry Smoothie

INGREDIENTS

serves 1
calories per
glass

93

1 eating apple, peeled, cored and chopped

2 tbsp chilled mineral water

55 g/2 oz fresh or thawed frozen raspberries

1 tsp clear honey (optional)

4 tbsp buttermilk or low fat natural yogurt

ice cubes

1 Put the apple in a smoothie machine or blender together with the mineral water and blend for 1 minute.

2 Reserve 2–3 raspberries for decoration and add the rest to the smoothie machine. Blend for 30 seconds before adding the honey, if using, and then add the buttermilk. Blend for a further minute.

3 Place a few ice cubes into a tumbler, pour over the smoothie, decorate with the reserved raspberries and serve.

Fresh Lemonade

**serves 4
(1.2 litres/
2 pints)**
calories per
300 ml/10 fl oz

82

INGREDIENTS

3 ripe lemons (preferably
organic or unwaxed)

115 g/4 oz caster sugar,
or to taste

850 ml/1½ pints boiling water

ice cubes

lemon slices, to decorate

1 Wash and thoroughly dry the lemons then, using a vegetable peeler, remove the rind from the lemons as thinly as possible. Reserve the lemons. Put the lemon rind into a heatproof bowl and sprinkle over the sugar. Pour over the boiling water, stir until the sugar has dissolved then cover loosely and leave until the liquid is cold.

2 Squeeze out all the juice from the lemons and pour into the cooled lemonade. Strain into a jug, check the sweetness and add a little more sugar if required.

3 Place some ice cubes in a tumbler, pour in the lemonade and decorate with a lemon slice. Serve.

Raspberry Crush

INGREDIENTS

serves 4
calories
per 300 ml/
10 fl oz

63

300 g/10½ oz fresh or thawed frozen raspberries

4 tbsp orange juice

1–2 tsp clear honey, or to taste

crushed ice

300 ml/10 fl oz soda water

4 scoops raspberry sorbet or frozen raspberry yogurt

1 Reserve a few raspberries for the decoration then put the remainder in a smoothie machine or blender. Switch on and with the motor running, add the orange juice and blend for 1 minute.

2 Add the honey to taste and blend for 20 seconds. Half-fill a tumbler with the crushed ice and top up with the soda water. Place a scoop of raspberry sorbet or frozen yogurt on top and serve decorated with the reserved raspberries.

Pineapple Crush

serves 4
calories
per 300 ml/
10 fl oz

52

INGREDIENTS

½ small ripe pineapple
(to give 225 g/8 oz of fresh
peeled pineapple)

2–3 tsp maple syrup, or to
taste

150 ml/5 fl oz orange juice

2 tsp ground ginger, or to taste

crushed ice

300 ml/10 fl oz American
ginger ale or chilled mineral
water

8 long chives

1 Place the pineapple on a chopping board and cut away the plume, skin and the base. Cut the pineapple into quarters and cut away the hard central core. Chop the flesh into small pieces.

2 Place a few pieces of pineapple in a smoothie machine or blender and blend for 1 minute. Add the maple syrup and about 50 ml/2 fl oz orange juice. With the motor running, add the remaining pineapple, a few pieces at a time, with a little more orange juice.

3 When all the pineapple and juice have been used, add the ground ginger and blend again briefly. Place some crushed ice in tumblers and fill with the pineapple juice. Top up with ginger ale, decorate with 2 chive lengths per glass and serve.

Low Fat Banana Shake

serves 1
calories per
portion

86

INGREDIENTS

55 g/2 oz ripe bananas, peeled
and cut into chunks

1 tsp maple syrup, or to taste

1 tsp ground cinnamon
(optional)

150 ml/5 fl oz skimmed milk

crushed ice

1 scoop low fat vanilla or
chocolate ice cream

sprinkle of grated chocolate
(optional)

1 Put the banana chunks in a smoothie
machine or blender, with maple syrup to
taste and ground cinnamon if using. Switch
on and with the motor running, add the milk
and blend for 1 minute, or until smooth.

2 Place some crushed ice in a tumbler and
pour the shake over. Add a scoop of low fat
vanilla or chocolate ice cream and serve
sprinkled with a little grated chocolate, if liked.

Summer Punch

serves 10
calories
per 150 ml/
5 fl oz glass

99

INGREDIENTS

75 cl bottle rosé wine, chilled

1 tbsp clear honey

150 ml/5 fl oz brandy (optional)

115 g/4 oz mixed summer berries, such as raspberries, blueberries and strawberries

3–4 fresh mint sprigs

600 ml/1 pint chilled sparkling water

8 ice cubes

1 Pour the wine into a punch bowl or large glass serving bowl. Add the honey and stir well. Add the brandy, if using.

2 Cut any large fruits into bite-sized pieces and place all the fruits and mint sprigs into the wine.

3 Leave to stand for 15 minutes then add the sparkling water and the ice cubes. Ladle the punch into glasses or punch cups ensuring each has an ice cube and a few pieces of fruit. Serve with a spoon to eat the fruit, if liked.

Winter Warmer

serves 10
calories
per 150 ml/
5 fl oz glass

99

INGREDIENTS

75 cl bottle red wine, such as claret

55 g/2 oz light soft brown sugar

2 cinnamon sticks, bruised, plus extra unbruised cinnamon sticks, to decorate (optional)

1 tsp allspice

4–6 whole cloves

1 small orange (preferably organic or unwaxed)

1 lemon (preferably organic or unwaxed)

150 ml/5 fl oz rum or brandy

300 ml/10 fl oz black tea, made from Darjeeling tea

1 Pour the red wine into a heatproof bowl and place over a saucepan of gently simmering water. Add the sugar with all the spices.

2 Cut the orange and lemon into thin slices, then add to the wine with the rum. Heat gently, stirring occasionally, for 15–20 minutes, or until the sugar has dissolved and the wine is hot.

3 Pour in the tea, heat for a further 10 minutes, then serve in heatproof glasses. Decorate the glasses with extra unbruised cinnamon sticks, if desired.

Index